MARKETING FOCUS

A Field Guide for Improving Marketing Operations

David Boroi

First Edition

Cover design: David Boroi
Copyright © 2016 by David Boroi

Ordering Information:
Quantity sales. Special discounts are available on quantity purchases by corporations, associations, and others. For details, contact the publisher at the address above.
Orders by U.S. trade bookstores and wholesalers. Please contact David Boroi: Tel: (614) 507-5327

Printed in the United States of America

ISBN 10 153730223X
ISBN 13 9781537302232

First Edition

To the ultimate focus of my life - my family, friends and colleagues.

Special thanks to some of my professional mentors over the years: Tom, Dave, Derrick, Joe, Brian, Maria and Kim.

Contents

EVOLVE to *ADAPT* to *CHANGE*   *140*

DELIVER for *CUSTOMER VALUE*   *165*

About the Author

Over the course of his career in Marketing, David has worn many hats from design and development to writing and planning to analytics and management. He's been fascinated by the challenge of trying to wrestle with the dynamic and sometimes elusive nature of planning and managing marketing in organizations. His hope in writing this book was to introduce some concepts that could help marketing professionals and managers reduce their stress levels and improve their business through better prioritization, organization, control, simplification, alignment and long-term sustainability.

Preface

The marketing function of most organizations continues to evolve at an exceedingly rapid pace. Primarily fueled by digital technologies, tools and trends, marketing teams are faced with a growing level of complexity in the way they operate. And with this complexity, comes an overwhelming number of choices and decisions, a need for speed to stay competitive, and ultimately higher levels of stress. There's also the problem with the inherent nature of how the marketing function is perceived and the typical makeup of its contributors. Part of its allure is the seemingly endless creative possibilities available for achieving growth or making an impact, as well as the need for experimentation as a means to better influence human behavior. The combination of increasing performance uncertainty, open-ended possibilities for strategic aim and rapid change of consumer preferences, can often lead to chaotic and uncontrolled environments. While some chaos is welcome and even necessary, not seeking to develop a more structured, sophisticated system or continuously striving to make operational improvements is a mistake.

The FOCUSED Framework (Filter, Organize, Control, Unify, Simplify, Evolve and Deliver) is a collection of concepts for helping a marketing team gain better focus on doing the work that really matters by achieving greater clarity, organization, control, alignment and sustainability

around activities and initiatives.

With more focus applied, distractions in marketing can be reduced. Distractions like spending too much time on administrative, low value activities, chasing too many new ideas and constantly reinventing the wheel.

While suited primarily for teams of many, the concepts of this book can be applied to teams of any size starting at one, simply scaling the approaches as necessary. This is not a comprehensive prescription, but rather a collection of tools and techniques to help you run marketing more efficiently and effectively.

Given the overwhelming number of choices and options for marketers today, a focused mind-set can help keep the sanity.

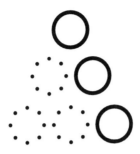

FILTER *for* CRITICAL AREAS *of* IMPACT

The role of leadership is to transform the complex situation into small pieces and prioritize them.

Carlos Ghosn

Because of today's rapidly changing business environment and seemingly endless marketplace of ideas, perspectives and opportunities, many marketing leaders are struggling to develop an evolving, clear and achievable set of priorities and targets. The result: organizational dysfunction, operational in-efficiency, unanticipated risk and/or missed opportunities.

The lack of proper prioritization of marketing initiatives can take a number of different forms including:

1. Going after too much.
2. Going after the wrong things.

Filter for Critical Areas of Impact

3. Re-inventing the wheel from discovery to execution.

4. Doing things that don't add customer value.

5. Not selecting activities that closely align to strategy and/or solve business problems.

6. Changing course too often and lacking follow-through.

To avoid these problems, the art and science of getting marketing FOCUSED starts with creating a strong and systematic ongoing prioritization process.

When using a process to **FILTER** marketing efforts, there's essentially three areas of consideration: backlog generation, scoring and prioritization. While these stages generally won't always occur in a linear fashion, they do require continuous grooming and refinement.

Backlog generation and refinement includes establishing clarity around 'all the things' your marketing organization wants to go after or is currently working on, from an operational, technical, organizational development and tactical perspective. Secondly, and equally important, it involves vocalizing and communicating this list to the broader organization or team and various stakeholders (this becomes part of the UNIFY process in a later chapter).

Scoring backlogged activities involves applying points to those backlog lists based on certain criteria. Simply, the higher the point value, typically the higher the priority. Low scoring

Filter for Critical Areas of Impact

items get filtered out for future consideration. There are generally four major areas to score your initiatives against.

Strategic Fit

Can these activities or initiatives be mapped to organizational or business goals, objectives, problems and KPI's? Is there alignment with other organizational function strategies?

Level of Impact

What value is being delivered to customers, internal or external? How is value competitively positioned and how will it impact revenue and other key performance indicators? Here we can look at various assumptions based on prior efforts, market research, qualitative and quantitative research and case studies.

Feasibility

Are the necessary resources available or is there a potential to go over budget and over capacity? Will it pass internal political interests?

It's likely you won't have all the answers here, but this will become a best estimate after working with other stakeholders and understanding relative capabilities.

Competency

Performed as part of a gap analysis, establish the organization's current level of maturity in the area relating to the particular initiative. Depending on your organization's approach or philosophy, initiatives within areas of lower maturity may be weighted higher as they are needed opportunities for improvement, or alternatively, weighted lower as they don't fall into your marketing's core or important competencies. There's a little bit of overlap here in competency with feasibility and strategic fit, however it may be beneficial to call out this seperately as it's own factor to provide a current state of affairs.

Finally, prioritization is the rank ordering and potential planning of those activities. It involves identifying the key areas or buckets in your marketing ecosystem (ie. dashboards, partners, sales enablement, software, etc.), mapping backlog activities to those key areas, reviewing against the four areas just mentioned and scoring appropriately. This can be a team and/or individual activity. An example of a short list is provided later in the chapter.

What gets initially included in the filtering process as ad hoc decision-making, unchecked experimentation and misaligned tactics, leaves as a smaller set of achievable initiatives that fit into alignment with larger business objectives. The goal is to create an ongoing, standardized process that fits into your organization's management frameworks.

Channel Evaluation

Depending on the level of sophistication of your organization or business, marketing communication is often the primary activity of a marketing function. However, if your marketing function plays a greater role in the entire product or service lifecycle, this may mean examaining channels for delivering your product and service to customers, partnership programs and front-line customer service. So, let's consider a more holistic approach that includes what's required to distribute an organization's brand message, products, services and value in the marketplace.

The channels you choose, therefore, and not choose for that matter, are critically important. Filtering out underperforming channels or activities within them can provide greater focus on the channels that can deliver the greatest impact.

Ultimately, you want to determine which channels best fit your

unique value proposition or strategy in the marketplace, and that will drive the greatest value to your firm and customers.

Some examples of channels to evaluate might include:

- E-commerce
- Partner networks
- Social media
- Sales and customer service teams
- Referrals
- Strategic relationships
- Advertising
- Brick and mortar experiences
- Co-marketing
- Advocacy groups

Filter for Critical Areas of Impact

- Influencers

- Digital properties

- Supply chains

- Franchises

- Affiliate sources

- Marketplaces

- Physical properties

- Events

Once you've identified all existing and potential channel opportunities, add all future and ongoing work to the backlog or current roadmap. You'll ultimately want a complete picture so you can map these against various areas of evaluation discussed later.

A Balanced Approach

Start by thinking of marketing as a microcosm

of a typical business with functional areas like production, engineering, operations, sales, finance, distribution, etc. To operate at its best, similar to how a business holistically operates, marketing must be able to examine and improve functions that reflect similar needs. For example:

- Content creation (production)
- Content promotion (distribution)
- Internal communication and buy-in (sales)
- Design and development around product support, content, delivery (engineering)
- Spend control (finance)
- Project and campaign management (operations)

A balanced approach should be used to address

each area and there should be an understanding of how each area impacts the other.

Use areas of imbalance or inefficiency to identify items for the backlog.

In other words, identify whether or not you're operating at full capacity on all fronts, and your particular areas of weakness. Or, conversely, if you're working at areas that don't matter. For example:

- Are there controls in place to balance spend and budget across all channels over time?
- Are there the right processes in place to ensure proper buy-in and evaluate a project's ROI?

- Does the product team have the right structure to deliver efficiently and effectively?
- Are the right technology solutions and people in place to execute against plans?

Imbalances in systems could be areas you want to address. Add them to the backlog.

Gap Analysis

Determine the current performance or the level of maturity of deploying the tactics in each area. Levels of maturity are discussed in more detail in the chapter on EVOLVING. A Radar chart can help visualize gaps between current compentency, peroformance or level of maturity in an area and the expected levels.

Filter for Critical Areas of Impact

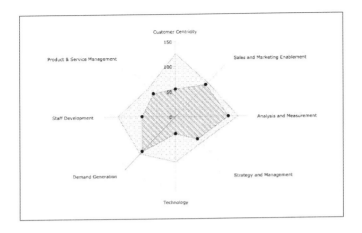

Backlog Development

Once you've established the channels you're currently using and plan to use, the areas you need to improve to operate effectively as a 'business' within your organization, the gaps within your current level of marketing maturity and the goals you want to achieve, it's time to get everything out on the table.

Work backwards to create a list of the tactical initiatives necessary to reach these objectives or solve these problems.

Organize them into 7-10 major categories, appropriate sub-categories and include all of your current activities in each category, as well as other potential initiatives you may deploy in the future. Some of the broad and corresponding sub-categories might include:

- **Customer Centricity:** research, service delivery processes, customer data, community management, satisfaction testing, experience design
- **Sales and Marketing Enablement:** marketing support of sales, cross-functional

Filter for Critical Areas of Impact

support of marketing

- **Analysis and Measurement:** access to tools, processes of measurement, frequency and depth of analysis, data delivery, dashboards
- **Strategy and Management:** planning process, objective and target scoping, budgeting approach, process management
- **Technology Enhancements:** digital capabilities, system integration, automation, project management
- **Product and Service Management:** training, competitive positioning, development process
- **Demand Generation:** offline and online marketing activities aimed at generating leads or customers
- **Training & Development:** training, recruiting, re-organization, succession planning, etc.

Evaluate and Prioritize

Now re-evaluate the backlog again based on strategic fit, level of impact, feasibility and competence to create an overall priority list. Give each a 0-5 score (or some other scoring reubric) based on degree of fit, impact and risk. Sum the scores from a priority perspective. Then filter the entire list by both lowest performance/maturity scores and highest priority. These become your potential areas of focus or 'big rocks' for the quarter, year, etc. This list can then be revisted and fed into your tools and processes for managing daily and weekly activity. More on this in a later section.

Scores could be in the 0-5 range and based on a combination of qualitative and quantitative data, or simply by using intuition and gut feel.

For example, a score of '1' would likely indicate very little effort or focus, whereas a score of '5' might reflect use of best-in-class practices or highest levels of performance.

You might enlist members of your team or other stakeholders to help provide feedback for either the qualitative or quantitative portion of your evaluation.

Filtering may require some additional up front research such as auditing channel effectiveness, stakeholder surveys, new research on audience preferences, etc.

Typical reasons to remove activities:

- Weak tie to business objectives
- Doesn't produce scalable results
- Low impact to customer value chain
- Not timely or can wait
- Level of effort unjustified

After establishing a baseline for the quarter or the year, you'll need some ongoing processes to re-evaluate and prioritize. Businesses and markets are in a constant flux, and you should change and adapt accordingly, just not blindly, or without purpose or team collaboration.

Additionally, some activities may have been identified as too risky, and need further validation to justify prioritization through piloting, prototyping or further research and evaluation. This activitiy may simply need adjusted and called out as a pilot or test.

On the next page is a sample matrix that could be used when conducting your evaluation and prioritization of marketing activities.

Key Area	Project / Activity / Initiative
Analysis & Measurement	Display metrics tied to revenue perfor-
Strategy & Management	Create a formal zero-based budget per
Strategy & Management	Build automated nurture sequence
Sales & Marketing Enablement	Develop playbooks for all product lines
Technology Enhancements	Build online portal for access to resources
Sales & Marketing Enablement	Develop an SLA
Demand Generation	Create online calculator
Demand Generation	Launch retargeting efforts
Customer Experience Design	Investigate and map support systems
Training & Development	Attend 1-2 industry conferences a year
Product & Service Management	Survey customers on innovative new
Technology Enhancements	Deploy new programmatic ad system
Analysis & Measurement	Conduct an audit of existing systems
Technology Enhancements	Implement new CRM system
Customer Centricity	Conduct customer survey across lines
Training & Development	Implement new staff training program
Technology Enhancements	Implement new automated workflows

Filter for Critical Areas of Impact

Competence	Strategic Fit	Impact	Feasibility	Priority
4	3	2	1	High
2	4	3	5	Low
3	2	3	3	Medium
2	3	4	2	Medium
2	3	2	1	Low
1	3	4	5	Low
3	4	2	1	Low
1	1	3	2	Low
2	3	4	5	High
5	4	5	3	High
3	4	2	1	Medium
4	5	2	3	Medium
3	4	5	5	High
4	5	5	4	High
3	2	2	2	Low
4	5	4	2	Medium

Filter for Critical Areas of Impact

Action Items

- ❑ Create a backlog of all unfinished activities and programs.

- ❑ Collect a thorough list of categorized best practices based on industry and other factors

- ❑ Develop categories and sub-categories for the work you do.

- ❑ Run a gap analysis to understand current capabilities against potential ideal state.

- ❑ Create a list of future and potential activities

- ❑ Rate activities by strategic fit, impact, competence and feasibility.

- ❑ Sort and produce a plan.

- ❑ Discuss ways with your team to ensure ongoing effectiveness prior to evaluation.

- ❑ Identify activities that require additional research or validation and re-prioritize.

ORGANIZE for GREATER CLARITY

The secret of all victory lies in the organization of the non-obvious.

Oswald Spengler

Organization brings greater clarity. Clarity brings more focus. And a marketing function, organized by its people and systems, needs clarity. But, to create a more organized marketing function, it requires creating structure, improving the flow of information and streamlining decision-making.

When priorities are established, they must be adopted into systems designed for effectively **ORGANIZING** the work. This requires examining team structures, management technology and planning methods.

Team Structures

Define roles and management structures and provide them in a visible format. There are generally six groups of specialization within markeitng including strategy, creative, development, research, media and communications, customer experience and analytics. Every organization, however, is different. The typical specialized areas within those groups might include:

- Product marketing

- Content strategy

- Creative specialization

- Demand generation

- Analytics and operations

- Upsell and renewal

- Customer experience

- Product marketing and management

- Media relations

- Web and mobile development

- Public speaking

- Sales and channel support

While dependent on strategy, industry and culture, appropriate functions will be organized by team size. Regardless, every member of the team should be aware of their responsibilities. The top trends in organizing a marketing team, as adapted from a recent HubSpot study, include the following styles:

- **Flexible** - A structure allows for adding head count and/or functions seamlessly as the company's product mix evolves.

- **Partial Funnel Focus** - A team built primarily to scale a portion of the marketing and sales funnel. For example a team focused on top-of-funnel ("ToFu") growth, may specialize primarily in content marketing as the largest group, followed by advertising and product marketing.

- **Full Funnel Focus** - a team grouped by stages of the marketing funnel, from awareness (seo, web, and creative design) to acquisition (conversion optimization, lead nurturing and sales enablement) to repeat (referral, affiliate and loyalty).

- **Product Focus** - Marketing activity primarily flows from product marketing managers to other specialists.

- **Culture Focus** - In this very flat structure, the entire organization is expected to be involved in the marketing process, and titles carry less meaning.

This process may also reveal gaps in existing structures or a weaker capacity in specialized areas. These can become additional areas to include the backlog.

Job Descriptions

Traditional marketing job analysis often produces job descriptions that fall short of compelling performance-based descriptions.

Descriptions that focus on skills and experience required don't effectively reach a larger, and potentially better, pool of talent.

Marketing job descriptions that focus on

performance measures and opportunities can produce better candidates, and ultimately better team members. Such descriptions include language around how the position will help to 'create, lead, change, manage or produce' meaningful outcomes for the organization.

Management Technology

Staying organized requires the right supporting software to keep information, people and objectives on track. Disorganized, under-utilized and inadequete technology implementations creates unnecessary administrative work. This takes away from focusing efforts on more important strategic activities.

Project Management Tools

The options to manage marketing activities vary greatly by the size of your organization, customization needs and how you operate with other functions in the organization. Project management tools ultimately should drive efficiencies in marketing operations. The features often present in these tools that help keep teams organized and focused on what matters includes:

- Automated workflows (ie. tasks and approvals)
- Calendars and timelines
- Project and task tracking
- Messaging and communication
- Software integrations
- Cost and budget tracking

Organize for Greater Clarity

- Permissions management

- Dashboards and reporting

- Customization capabilities

- Mobile access

- Interface usability and user experience

- Services, support, vendors and community

Evaluate what matters to your team with internal and external interviews, time studies (where do inefficiencies exist), mandatory requirements analysis and cost/benefit analysis work. Leave room for future growth, but pick the features and functionalities that matter most and focus on getting those right first. There are a lot of options out there, but here are a few to consider:

- Workfront

- Workzone

- Wrike

- Jira

- Redbooth

- Brightpod

- MavenLink

- CoSchedule

Create a vendor matrix that looks at current and desired capabilities and maps to each of the above solutions. Look for opportunities to reduce redundancies between current toolsets. Also, consider what processes can be streamlined and how that can be factored into the return on investment in software purchases.

Asset Management Systems

Manage and organize content assets in a database

system to ensure clarity around ownership, revision dates, location, potential gaps, etc. It can be organized around products or services and type of content, or whatever makes sense for your environment. It should be accessible by all members of the organization to assist with locating relevant documents, web pages, videos, etc. The key is to treat your content like any other business asset.

It took time, money and resources to produce it, so why let it collect dust?

Like any other asset, it often requires regular maintenance, updates and polishing. A single data source of these assets gives you the ability to report on, search for and filter a list of what's been published, requires review or needs created. Each asset record could include:

- Title
- Publish date
- Last modified date
- Subject matter expert
- Status (assigned, work-in-progress and review, published)
- Category (testimonial video, post, white paper, e-book, FAQ's)
- Other important meta data

Asset Categorization

Modeling the categories, styles, and types of messaging required for market success within the buyer's journey can mean creating media formats and content types that address:

- Demand creation

- Meeting creation

- Opportunity creation

- Order creation

- Urgency creation

Mapping assets to these situations can ensure there's an adequate amount of both descriptive and persuasive communications. This often requires a great deal of alignment, as discussed in Chapter 4.

Marketing Knowledgebase

To develop greater competence around products and services, a central repository of information, ideally online, can serve as an important tool for faster and higher quality content development, consistent new hire onboarding and opportunities for continuous learning. It's especially important in organizations with complex products and services and marketing needs.

Too many dependencies on other internal staff members can create bottlenecks. These bottlenecks can prevent focus on what's important.

Social Business

Managing the flow of information is key to preventing bottlenecks, developing internal knowledge and improving quality. Often email inboxes, file networks and chat platforms create silos of information and context. Social business tools, however, are platforms designed to get you out of your inbox, directory and chat window and onto one platform.

Part social media, part intranet, part wiki, these platforms are the next one-stop shop for marketers, vendors, internal and external partners to collaborate, share information, manage projects and exchange ideas.

Many believe they are the next evolution of email and corporate chat technology, as they essentially combine these communication tools into one, and provide other enhanced features that eliminate internal corporate networks and file repositories. run polls, upload files, create workspaces, events and tasks, etc. Out of

Organize for Greater Clarity

the email inbox, social chat window, internal network drive and project management application, and into one tool.

Its central premise is to divide work into what they call spaces, groups of conversations, tasks, events, etc. that tie to an organization function or broader topic. These workspaces can be divided further into a web-based folder structure, containing relevant conversations, all of which can be tagged and then searched and filtered. The marketing space can be divided into areas around planning, partnerships and campaigns.

Operations can invite vendors, contractors and consultants into appropriate spaces to expand their team's capacity.

Marketing can create conversations with members of the organization before each meeting for everyone to capture ideas and action items real-time for future reference. Some tools on the market that are receiving praise in this area include:

- Jive

- Kona

- Facebook Workplace

- Slack

- Jostle

Refine Calendars

Find a central place to manage all date-based activities and use color-coding and labels to differentiate the different types of events. This central calendar will be updated based on the frequency of your meeting and planning process and style of management. Ideally, this calendar will be fully integrated with your entire marketing suite, allowing you to directly tie production elements, metrics and team members in one place, giving a complete time-based picture of marketing efforts.

Campaigns

Campaigns typically include all the calendar items together, or can be identified within each calendar item record, in order to associate asset production, events, product launches, etc. into this broader category—important for tracking campaign-level impact and help to organize these smaller activities thematically. Knowing when a campaign begins and ends brings clarity to everyone involved, including other stakeholders in the organization.

Anchors or Milestones

Identify key events or time periods throughout the year. Types may include:

- Company events
- Buying seasons (typical periods of interest to buyers)
- Product launches
- Time-sensitive annual deadlines

This may help in selecting the types of campaigns, assets and events you plan.

Editorial Calendars

As Marketing continues to become the

"publishing" resource of organizations, the tools used by media companies to organize their content production become more relevant to marketing managers.

A common example is the classic editorial calendar, which helps you schedule and assign content asset production and promotion.

- **Frequency:** Determine the level of production of content assets
- **Schedule:** Schedule weekly, monthly and quarterly production of assets by type
- **Asset Briefs:** Develop single-page briefs for assets to develop quarterly
- **Assigning External Resources:** Allocate subject matter experts where appropriate

Also, overlay on your editorial calendar various organization events to plan, promote and execute. You don't want to lose sight of key external events that could impact performance or become opportunities to fill customer needs.

Buyer's Journey

A careful analysis and mapping of the path in which a prospect or customer becomes a buyer, can provide clarity around where to devote efforts. It also provides a higher level of understanding around key points of interaction that may require rethink or redesign. Organizing your buyer's journey in a clearly visible format can provide better visibility to the team for discovering these opportunities.

Once mapped for various product

and service lines, with an understanding the every customer path and entry point will be different, you can map content, assets and experiences for each stage of the journey.

Find gaps within the customer experience where marketing can improve delivery and execution. And look for ways to streamline or simplify the customer's ability to get from point A to point B. Organizing all touchpoints a prospect or customer experiences can help identify areas that need greater focus.

Strategic Planning

Annual Plan

While the old days of developing a heavily

documented, 3-5 year marketing plan are nearly over, annual planning is still necessary for establishing a clear picture of overall marketing realities, strategies and initiatives. Some of the areas to include are:

- Situational considerations (any market conditions to factor)
- Budgets
- Objectives, Priorities, Goals and Strategies
- Major Initiatives and Campaigns
- Projections and Forecasting

An annual plan should serve as a guide, not a rigid, verbouse plan. It should be a living, breathing document that gets re-focused and adjusted as the market and business changes.

Business Objectives

What should the marketing function of your business or organization achieve—increased demand, a new perception in your market, more awareness for your products and services, a better feedback loop for engineering, etc. If this isn't clear or fully understood, begin to map out marketing's link to business objectives.

Business objectives are the quantifiable targets a company needs to achieve. They may tie to revenue and customer base growth, market share, profitability and operational efficiences. Primary marketing priorities, goals and strategies must map back to these key objectives.

Marketing Priorities

Marketing must decide where and how it can

impact these business objectives. The next step is to outline what priorities marketing can reasonable handle based on capacity and timing. These priorities become the top areas of focus for marketing leadership.

Marketing Goals

Marketing goals turn the priorities into quantifiable statements. They will be different for every organization and requires some conversations with your leadership team and other stakeholders. Get specific and reasonable about the results you want to achieve: ie. $10 million in additional revenue.

Some goal areas might include:

- Increase sales
- Generate leads (or opportunities)

- Acquire new customers

- Reduce churn (or retain customers)

- Increase up-sells and cross-sells (higher transaction values)

- Improve awareness

- Increase customer satisfaction

- Launch a new product or solution

- Re-brand or re-position.

- Increase web traffic

- Refine go-to-market strategy

- Launch a new initiative

- Improve use of a technology

Stay organized around a set of a few realistic and achievable goals.

Marketing Strategy & Tactics

Strategy defines the approach marketing will

take to hit its defined goals, while maintaining focus on the priorities. Tactics then become the specific actions that will be taken to achieve that strategy.

Develop Meeting Structures

Organize meetings around a format that is conducive to giving your meetings a purpose and produces greater clarity around goals and objectives. A sample agenda (see 'Agile Marketing' section on alternative versions) might include:

- Good News – 5 minutes
- Review KPI's/Scorecard – 5 minutes
- Big Rocks Review – 5 minutes
- Review Team Closed/Open Activity List – 10 minutes

- IDS (Issues. Discuss. Solve.) + Create activities – 45 min
- Conclude - 5 min

Repeatable and consistent meeting structures can keep the conversation focused on important issues at hand without too much divergance into unrelated and unimportant issues.

Action Items

Tackle some of these action items to get started on your way to a better organized marketing machine and structure.

- ❑ Set-up cross-functional meetings to establish clear and shared definitions.
- ❑ Audit technology stack to discover ways to more tightly integrate data.

- ❏ Move to a one-stop shop technology platform, where appropriate.
- ❏ Establish regular meetings with functions like sales to uncover meaningful ways to collaborate.
- ❏ Seek out tools and technology that empowers other functional areas.
- ❏ Maintain use of a strong calendar system.
- ❏ Organize content around the customer and buyer experience.
- ❏ Organize your strategy into an organic annual and quarterly plan.
- ❏ Refine your organizational chart based on your culture and strategy. Identify gaps in capability and competence.
- ❏ Revisit your job descriptions and seek to create performance based descriptions vs. simply more traditional roles and

responsibilities.

- ❑ Establish reoccurring meetings with a basic structure.

- ❑ Organize digital content and assets into a tracking system that is searchable and accessible across the organization.

- ❑ Categorize and tag assets in such a way that you can identify gaps and ensure accountability.

- ❑ Set up tools and systems organize information around organizational expertise and internal processes.

- ❑ Deploy modern applications that provide better organization of internal communication and projects.

CONTROL *AGAINST the DISTRACTIONS*

Control your own destiny or someone else will.

Jack Welch

Just as distractions impact individual performance, they can also impact organizational outcomes. The very nature of marketing's typical role in organizations today lends itself to being prone to higher levels of distraction. The need to constantly create new things and predict human behavior often leads to moving in too many directions, under-resourced initiatives and ultimately a seemingly out-of-control or unaccountable system. This isn't to say that some ambiguity, experimentation and ad hoc activity shouldn't be acceptable. Too much, however, is a recipe for mediocre results. Using Pareto's principle, assume 80% of activity should be tightly controlled and monitored, whereas 20-30% should be left for innovation, experimentation and testing new ideas.

Dashboard Design

Dashboards paint a picture of how marketing is performing. An incomplete picture means important areas are out of focus. The right amount of data that creates insight, organized in a such a way that is easily accessible in one place and understood by all stakeholders, brings clarity to performance. It allows for necessary adjustments to future filters on priority. Dashboards might communicate:

- Projects in progress
- Activities in progress or backlogged
- Monthly, quarterly and annual performance

measures

- Cross-functional comparative data
- Data designed to drive insights
- Data designed to show progress over time

Marketing dashboards should be split based on levels of granularity often into three general categories: impact on revenue generation and/or firm-wide performance, benchmark against quarterly and annual KPI's and analysis of softer metrics such as traffic, engagement and satisfaction. While tempting to use dashboards simply as a means for touting success (vanity metrics), they should serve as an important tool for assessing areas of strength or weakness, uncovering insights, diagnosing problems and keeping your team on the same page. Types of metrics to track by funnel stage include:

- **Awareness or attraction** - social engagement, impressions, visits, video views
- **Consideration** - leads generated, demos viewed, cost per lead, pricing pages viewed, buying guides downloaded, subscriptions
- **Conversion** - sales, acquisition cost, profit, transactions, average order value
- **Loyalty** - repeat purchases, Net Promoter Score (NPS), accounts created

Agile Management

Without going into great detail on adopting the framework to managing marketing initiatives and projects, agile is a powerful way to keep control on time and resources. The core values of agile marketing according to the Agile

Marketing manifesto include:

- Validated learning over opinions and conventions
- Customer focused collaboration over silos and hierarchy
- Adaptive and iterative campaigns over Big-Bang campaigns
- The process of customer discovery over static prediction
- Flexible vs. rigid planning
- Responding to change over following a plan
- Many small experiments over a few large bets

Some of the key aspects of moving to an agile framework include regular testing of hypothesis, prioritizing a backlog, a regular communication cadence and capturing learning. Creating variations to a purist agile framework are acceptable and can allow it to better fit into the context of how a particular organization or team operates.

Developing User Stories

Create high-level statements that capture what a prospect, customer or visitor does or needs from interacting with your company. It is often written in the following form:

As a <role or type of user> I want to <some desire or goal> so I can <some benefit>.

The user story brings context by specifying the who, how and why. It helps you frame the experience you are going to deliver in a way that gives value. And it helps you 'get in the head' of the user, customer or potential buyer. Frame your backlog in the context of user stories. An example user story might be this:

As an HR Director, I want the ability to learn about new approaches and techniques around people analytics, so that I can better leverage employee data to uncover insights.

While there are different schools of thought on how user stories can be organized, a common approach is to combine user stories into Epics, or essentially larger user stories. For example, the above example might be part of an Epic like:

As an HR Director, I want the ability to learn about trends and techniques in the HR function, so that I can improve our company's ability to manage people.

Ultimately, the specific technique you use isn't as important as the fundamental need to frame your activities around producing assets that deliver value to your audience. In the upcoming sections, you'll explore how you can test and prove these assumptions, as well as manage them to ensure efficient execution.

Prioritizing the Backlog

As discussed in the first chapter, the backlog is where all of the unstarted tasks, ideas and wishful-thinking is stored. On a regular cadence, such as during what is called a biweekly sprint, the backlog is re-examined for activities to complete and test during the next sprint.

Estimating

Part of planning out a sprint involves estimating the duration of team tasks. It's important to note that often 20% of work time can be devoted to unforeseen activities and projects, which can gradually be minimized over time. During sprint planning the team will assign a number from the Fibonacci sequence (e.g. 1, 2, 3, 5, 8, 13, 21, 34, etc.) to each high priority task based on it's relative size, given time estimates are too arbitrary. If a task is larger than 21 points, it is broken down into smaller tasks. Time is tracked during the sprint to determine the actual time to complete tasks in a burn-down chart, giving a better estimate for the next sprint.

Hypothesis Testing

Testing is a critical competent of agile

management. It may start with a couple test a week. By creating a hypothesis that may involve design updates, exploring new channels or changes to tactics, key learnings can be uncovered from analyzing the outcomes of these tests during the sprint. The goal is to then to accelerate this testing to impact the speed of growth.

Spend Control

Budgets

Budgeting gives you oversight on spend across all of your initiatives and gives you better control for making future adjustments based on spend to impact analysis. There are generally three basic types of budgets:

- **Zero-based** - price out all the tactics in your marketing plan to produce a total budget requirement.

- **Goals-based** - use past budgets and results to determine future budgets.

- **Product-based** - allocate time and spend towards particular products or service lines.

Track actual spend versus budgeted amounts and monitor how much is spent against total sales or revenue. Dependent on an organization's size, industry and maturity, it's anywhere from 3 - 15%. Use budgeting tools to monitor remaining spend, tie to product or service lines and gain insights into return on investment. With the number of options and directions to take, budgeting can help create a framework to reduce spending on distractions.

Control Against Distractions

The 70/20/10 Rule

A broad measure when allocating your mix of spend can use this moving target. Allocate 70 percent of the budget to tested and proven channels, with 20% allocated to channels that seem promising despite amount of evidence, and 10% allocated to experimental efforts. Ultimately, allow enough flexibility to adjust tactical execution when possible.

Attribution Modeling

According to a Forrester Research report on attribution modeling: "Traditional one-to-one, last-touch methods of allocating demand to marketing efforts are outdated and lead to a suboptimal marketing mix. Customer Intelligence (CI) professionals must adopt a cross-channel attribution model in order to optimize marketing budgets, accurately calculate customer value and acquisition costs, and develop a holistic view of the marketing ecosystem. Failure to embrace this new standard is expensive — firms will be plagued with continued channel conflict and an inefficient marketing budget." Being able to understand the true performance of different channels, both offline and online, can help marketers allocate marketing investments. Highly dependent on the type of organization, amount of data available and persistence of customer identifier, different types of attribution can be used including:

- **Linear** - Assign equal value across each interaction point.
- **Position-based** - Assign custom values

Control Against Distractions

to various points of interaction based on importance.

- **U-Shaped** - Greatest value assigned to the first touch and lead creation touch points (e.g. 30%) and distributing the remaining to others points.

- **W-Shaped** - Include the opportunity creation point after the lead creation point and distribute the remaining value equally.

- **Time Decay** - Assign most value to interactions closest to the sale.

Setting up your analytics for accurate attribution modeling will require some up-front time and effort, but can provide a foundational baseline for how you optimize and control your various channels.

Content and Style Guidelines

A thorough and detailed set of guidelines around all content production and publication provides a clear and focused framework for content creation and management. Ultimately, making small to large decisions around style, can eliminate having to constantly make decisions later which leads to inefficiencies. Furthermore, the level of consistency in your brand ecosystem, can either positively or adversely impact customer perception. Content guidelines provide a framework for:

- Visual styles and templates
- Website elements
- Branding
- Writing voice and tone

Control Against Distractions

- Contribution suggestions

- Typography, colors and image styles

- Logo usage

- Communication hierarchy

Create a central web-based location for guidelines to be accessed by everyone in the organization.

Automated Systems

Automation helps to not only reduce administrative burden, but also control processes to ensure consistency and eliminate missed opportunities. Some means of automation include:

- Drip email content based on areas of interest
- Triggered workflows

- Social media bulk scheduling

- Routine task automation

- Alerting of staff based on website behavior

- Emails triggered by site behavior (i.e. cart abandonment)

- Report delivery or creation

- Dynamic website content

Workflows

An important component of marketing automation, workflows help marketers to ensure the delivery of communication, reduce administrative time and effort and create consistent processes. Controlling the delivery of communication, task creation or maintenance of data, lets marketers stay focused on more strategic initiatives and scale existing systems. Some more specific use cases include:

- Nurture campaigns

- Ongoing A/B tests

- Schedule publications

- Follow-up workflow communication

- Monitor for customer feedback and complaints

- Hyperpersonalized content

- Automated customer onboarding

- Behavioral insights by alerts

- Post purchase drip campaign

- Segmentation by behavior

Campaign Definitions

Marketing software solutions provide a number of different means to manage campaigns. However, ensuring you capture all the necessary, relevant information on the who, what, why, when and where for a particular campaign can lead to better execution and control of results. Here's what you might capture:

- **Naming Convention** - Maintain name structure for sorting and organization (e.g. {Date} | {Offer, Product or Service} | {Target Audience}

- **ID** - Using a campaign ID might be useful for tracking identifiers used in link parameters

- **Campaign Type** - Identify the type of campaign for clarity on activities to be run and to determine variance among all campaigns. Might include: account-based, up-sell, cross-sell, re-engagement, referral, partner marketing, branding, etc.

- **Promotional Channels** - Decide on which

channels will be used. Might include: paid search, paid social, tradeshow, display, email, association, telemarketing, influences, etc.

- **Target Type** - Include the type of target audience such as partner, influencer, customer, affiliate

- **Related Assets** - Connect related content

- **Related Products / Services** - Describe products and solutions related to the campaign

- **Time Frame** - Provide a proposed start and end date

- **Budget** (actual/proposed) - Determine spend and provide data on actual spend

- **Activities** - Create a list of activities necessary to carry out the campaign including its owners. Build these into a backlog if using agile practices.

- **Lists** - Include the list of targeted accounts or contacts

- **Offer Type and Description** - Describe the type of offer such as a tool, download, research report, guide, webinar, consultation, demo, kit, etc.

- **Marketing Stage** - Describe stage in the marketing/sales funnel such as awareness, engagement, purchase and advocacy

- **Expected & Actual Results** - Describe the results of the campaign in numbers

Agreements

Documented and agreed upon agreements provide clarity in relationships and prevent distractions as the result of the redundancy of work, unclear objectives and fading levels of commitment from both parties.

Co-Marketing

Partnering up with other companies and agencies to market products and services can produce mutually beneficial results and allow organizations to focus on their strengths such as content development or a distribution channel.

A formalized co-marketing agreement can help define and control all aspects of a co-marketing relationship, like responsibilities, expenditures and more. Sharing the workload, especially by focusing on areas of strength, can reduce costs, scale results and expand reach.

Strategic Partnerships

Other types of partnerships can produce similar results, where each party identifies areas to collaborate and extend capacity. Again, a written agreement ensures a smoother working relationship.

Team Charters

Creating a written charter for your marketing team can help to ensure you stay focused on several key areas. For example, marketing operations might include:

- Defining strategy and aligning initiatives, metrics, people and tasks with the firm's business outcomes
- Developing and implementing metrics, infrastructure, and business processes
- Defining and managing systems and tools
- Establishing and communicating best practices

- Managing the budget and budgeting process
- Deploying technology to support performance measurement and reporting
- Working with the Marketing leadership team in the development of Marketing plans
- Supporting personnel to ensure team is focused on and measuring their contribution to Marketing objectives, strategies, programs and activities
- Monitoring and reporting on Marketing's progress against performance targets and detecting gaps and problems.

Similar to roles and responsibilities for an employee, this charter can serve as a reminder of the areas that need addressed over time, for each specific team within the marketing department or the function as a whole.

Process Documentation

Just like managing any other business function, documenting processes in marketing ensures consistent execution and eliminates time wasted on deciding how things get done. Change is inevitable and documenting everything becomes administrative burden. But, by focusing on tasks for specialists, especially in roles that have potential for churn, process documentation can reduce training costs and eliminate errors. Create easily accessibly (web-based) procedures with images and easy-to-follow workflow instructions. See the section in 'knowledgebase' and 'social business.'

Questionnaires and Templates

When developing a new service or product page, sales sheet, press release, post, etc.

having a template document containing the appropriate questions and fields helps ensure the right content is captured. Not having this as a guide leads to inconsistencies and a focus away from the quality of the subject matter.

Planning Checklists

Similar to process documentation, checklists provide a set of steps to complete an activity. Building checklists into team management software as a series of tasks for common activities, standardizes work, eliminates missed opportunities, reduces errors and keeps a focus on the quality of the work, not the process. On the other hand, checklists that are separated from tools for managing daily activities creates silos of information. More on this topic in the next chapter.

ROI Benchmarks

At the crux of a sustainable marketing program is being able to produce quantifiable results. Challenges to produce accurate numbers, however can be overcome over time by starting from a set of simple calculations. Ongoing focus on these numbers can provide opportunities for additional budget, greater buy-in and reinforced enthusiasm. Some of the core calculations might include:

- ROMI (Return on Marketing Investment) = (Sales Growth – Marketing Investment) / Marketing Investment
- Customer Acquisition Cost = Total Sales and Marketing Cost / Number of New Customers

Reporting

Creating a series of custom reports to relate to KPI's and the metrics that tie to them will evolve data analysis and maintenance capabilities. Heuristic research methods can serve as a starting point to uncover the questions that matter, and in turn the reports necessary to answer those questions. Data without the right questions to ask, is just data. Some questions you might ask include:

- How do we attribute a specific channel to sales outcomes?
- Is anyone using this part of the website?
- Has our demand generation quantity and quality improved since last year?
- What are the demographics of those

converting on the website?

With the right questions asked, now the right reports can be created.

Ongoing Audits

To find out if your strategy is working, you need to conduct regular audits that take an honest, objective, and critical look at what you are doing in order to evaluate the effectiveness of your programs, control for better outcomes and focus on the right areas that need improvement.

Conducting a Quarterly Audit

Re-evaluate various activities and initiatives at a regular cadence. Some goals might be to:

- Check engagement rates against benchmarks or goals set
- Evaluate strengths, weaknesses and opportunities based on data
- Comparatively A/B test any changes where applicable
- Evaluate each stage of your funnel and focus on the metrics that are leading indicators for sales

Conducting an Annual Audit

When possible, the marketing audit is generally best conducted by a third party, not a member of an organization. It should be:

- **Comprehensive** - covers all the areas of marketing function
- **Systematic** - an orderly analysis and

evaluation of firm's micro & macro environment, marketing principles, objectives, strategies and other operations that directly or indirectly influences the firm's marketing performance

- **Periodical** - instead of only when problems occur, audits should be conducted regularily

Components of a Marketing Audit

Consider some of the following areas to review:

- **Macro-Environment** - all the factors outside the firm that influences the marketing performance. (ie. Demographic, Economic, Environmental, Political, and Cultural.)
- **Task Environment** - The factors impacting the efficiency and effectiveness of marketing including Markets, Customers, Competitors,

Control Against Distractions

Distributors and Retailers, Facilitators and Marketing Firms, Public etc.

- **Marketing Strategy** - Examining the feasibility of Business Mission, Marketing Objectives and Goals and Marketing Strategies that have a direct impact on the firm's marketing performance.

- **Marketing Organization** - Evaluating the performance of staff at different levels of hierarchy.

- **Marketing Systems** - Maintaining and updating several marketing systems such as Marketing Information System, Marketing Planning System, Marketing Control System and New-Product Development System

- **Marketing Productivity** - Evaluating the performance of the Marketing activities in terms of Profitability and Cost-Effectiveness

- **Marketing Function** - Keeping a check on firm's core competencies such as Product, Price, Distribution, Marketing Communication and Sales Force.

As discussed in the first chapter on FILTERING, discoveries here might also be included as backlogged items for prioritization. Additionally, the audit may become a reoccuring activity within your roadmap.

Ad Management

With the number of available channels and the capability to refine, optimize and better target on these channels increasing, so does the complexity in managing it all. New tools like AdStage give marketers the ability to create, optimize and report on ads across several networks. Advertising has gone from a being a tactic for achieving broad reach in a marketplace to a narrow reach across a variety of channels. Attempting to narrowly target an audience in one or a few channels, may not prove worthwhile. Instead, a modern ad approach should consider employing all possible channels, given the wide variety of personal preferences for information consumption. Tight controls on costs are maintained by first deploying small tests to establish a baseline of data to inform additional spend. Streamlined visibility is key here as not only do you need to optimize within a channel, but also across various channels. And you can't assume a channel has no viability without sufficient data. The keys then to manage ads are as follows:

- Use a tool that gives visibility and control over all or most channels

- Start with small tests across all channels to accumulate data

- Control spend with narrow targeting, optimization techniques, budgeting, bid strategies, regular monitoring and employing general implementation best practices

- Leverage retargeting capabilities to strengthen and reinforce messaging

Meeting Cadence

How often you meet depends on the size and depth of your marketing function. If you're using agile methodologies, daily or weekly 15 minute morning stand ups might be appropriate. You might meet biweekly, or quarterly to review bigger rocks. The key is to develop a schedule and stick-to-it. For those that can't attend meetings, where it makes sense, a progress update should be provided.

Action Items

Time to take control. Here are some next steps.

❑ Create a list of questions to aid in the creation or refinement of dashboards for various levels of the organization and stage of the marketing funnel.

❑ Consider adopting agile methodologies vs. traditional project management methodologies.

❑ Trial agile and begin with team education and choosing a project or campaign to experiment with using the framework.

❑ Examine important activities that can be

automated using technology. Understand areas where your technology stack can and can't support it. Backlog future activities.

- [ ] Move to a one-stop shop technology platform, where appropriate, or seek out seamless integrations where gaps exist.

- [ ] Create a system to document processes.

- [ ] Refine or develop a thorough set of content/ brand guidelines.

- [ ] Better control marketing spend. Build out attribution models, better means of tracking, methods of optimization, focus of spend and budgeting practices.

- [ ] Control campaign scope with clear definitions. Manage a single data source.

- [ ] Create formal agreements with strategic partners.

- [ ] Develop reusable internal questionnaires

and templates to control information gathering and activity completion.

❑ Manage ad ROI with advanced control measures.

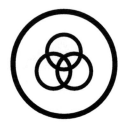

UNIFY *to* DEEPEN CONCENTRATION

The point here is that every organization, if it wants to create a sense of alignment and focus, must have a single top priority in a given time period.

Patrick Lencioni

At its core, marketing includes everything from products and services, distribution systems and pricing structures to sales models, advertising and engineering innovation. Marketing touches all areas of the organization, as it ultimately serves as the gateway for how value is delivered to and perceived by the customer. Realistically, marketing typically serves a more limited role in most organizations. It may be focused on communication and advertising, for example. Either way, just like any other business function (and arguably more so) it requires a tight integration with sales, engineering, finance, support and leadership. And moreover, it requires an alignment with both seen and unrecognized customer wants, needs, frustrations, pain points, etc.

Customer Alignment

Creating true customer alignment begins with bringing together representatives from product or service development, customer service, marketing, sales, etc. to define buyer and advocacy personas and the customer journey and experience. Marketing can segment initiatives, content and even teams by customer personas. Ultimately, all business activities can be derived from these journeys, aligning everything the business does from advertising to accounts receivable to a customer experience touchpoint.

Unify to Deepen Concentration

Creating journey maps begins with adequete research using:

- Surveys
- Focus groups
- Interviews (internal and external)
- Market and consumer research
- Analytics

Specific points on the journey can be mapped to marketing activities to ensure the gaps and opportunities are identified. Each area should have some measurable KPI's to improve, and subsequently the size of impact understood for each for proper FILTERING. While traditionally personas are seen as collections of customer attributes like demographic, psychographics, etc, they can become further segmented by behavior-based groupings. A single persona might contain groups thats are new to the brand, loyal customers, interested in specific product lines and buy at different frequencies.

Strategic Alignment

At its core, marketing should tie directly to key business objectives and, where appropriate, influence these directives.

Definitions

Often departments and functions may have a different meaning for what things are and how they should be done. This misalignment can cause breakdowns in communication and collaboration. By coming together to discuss

Unify to Deepen Concentration

and form clear definitions with contributions from all stakeholders, everyone is on the same page. This may include creating a clear and shared definition around:

- Customer lifecycle stages
- Buyer personas
- Shared key performance indicators
- Product and service messaging
- Lead hand-off process
- Progression of a lead

Service-level Agreements

Create a shared document between sales and marketing that outlines important definitions and accountability measures. First, include the key definitions described previously. Second, create some shared goals around sales measures.

Break down the sales metrics into meaningful goals around lead generation. Metrics that can be monitored might include:

- Lead response time
- Lead to customer close percentage
- Sales deal size
- Percent of revenue generated from marketing leads

Document accountability measures on both sides and meet to discuss.

Approval Workflows

Ensuring all stakeholders involved in a campaign are on the same page can be challenging. There are a number of tools that can improve this process including ProofHQ and Workfront.

Unify to Deepen Concentration

Getting sign-off on ideas, dates, copy, creative, etc. in a streamlined and consistent process prevents errors, increases buy-in and improves communication.

Team Alignment

Sales

According to a 2011 Aberdeen Group study, highly aligned organizations achieved an average of 32% year-over-year revenue growth – while their less aligned competitors saw a 7% decrease in revenue. Yet according to another study from Forrester, just 8% of companies say they have tight alignment between sales and marketing. There are several reasons why better alignment might be necessary:

- Conflicts are evident

- Lack of clear definitions on shared processes

- Efforts duplicated

- Competition for funding

- Limited understanding of sales function by marketing or vice versa

- Lack of consistent cross-communication

Techniques such as account-based marketing that are gaining popularity and are the result of both improvements of digital technologies, as well as the recognition that sales and marketing should be working closer together. Tools like DemandBase allow marketers to specific IP addresses of target accounts with highly personalized advertising. One such example is a firm that hypertargeting all their whitepaper content to corporate employees at 'Walmart'

Unify to Deepen Concentration

spending ad dollars only on that account.

Spending budget evenly across all potential and current customers might not be the best way to allocate resources. Focusing more spend on best performing accounts can produce better ROI. Account-based marketing tactics and technologies allow marketing and sales to work closer together to target accounts that have the highest potential to produce greater returns. Part of your technology infrastructure to enhance alignment might include solutions like:

- Display Targeting and Retargeting
- Customer Intelligence Management
- Account Planning Management
- Data Services

- Customer Success Management
- Programmatic Advertising

Engineering

While many of the activities managed by Marketing and Engineering are quite different, there is often a need to work together on product development. Marketing often takes concern with consumer preferences and competitor positioning, whereas engineering may look more closely at feasibility and robustness of the product. For the best outcome on product design, both approaches should be considered concurrently. Silos can be broken down with regular, meaningful dialogue between product managers and product marketers

Vendors, Agencies & Contractors

Keeping channel partners, vendors, agencies, suppliers and contractors aligned with the goals and objectives of marketing reduces errors, overspend and missed opportunities.

Developing clear and well-defined briefs and requirements is critical for ensuring successful engagements with agencies and contractors. Standardized and structured requests for information ensures the right information is captured every time. By providing portals or hubs to external collaborators that serve as a central source of information, makes sure there's adequate knowledge transfer. Secondly, it's important to manage accountability. External providers should be able to demonstrate how they deliver and measure what is expected. Finally, seek to develop a long-term relationship.

New agency or vendor reviews divert attention from concentrating on marketing activities.

Channel Partners

Related organizations that sell, market or implement your products or services should be treated as extensions of your marketing efforts. Therefore, delivery excellence requires the same considerations as aligning internal functions. Marketing programs through channel partners should be structured in a way where there is sufficient enablement across the channel partner's capacity for sales, production, delivery, etc. Additionally, all marketing assets, tools, knoweldge and resources transferred to the channel partner should meet the standards of excellence as any internal delivery. Clearly define the amount of effort needed to effectively enable channel partners, and then make sure there are enough resources to sustain this strategy. Some questions to ask include:

- What are the essential business drivers for the channel partner and how can your product enable (align to) those drivers?
- Are there areas to work together to align resources to optimize spending?
- Do you see any changes in direction from the channel partner? Is there a gap of alignment in service delivery method, solution or toolset?
- Are the partner's existing capabilities and resources in technology and operations sufficient to support growth?
- Do you have the right level of relationship with the channel partner to be able to assess

the wants and needs of a customer (not owned by you)?

- Are you aligned to mutual metrics with channel partners?

Integrated Systems

Fully-integrated platforms that leverage automation can reduce administrative burden and provide a central, focused control center for tracking marketing efforts. The availability of hundreds of tools, silo'd data and disjointed processes can often add unnecessary layers of complexity, lead to errors, missed opportunities and increased production time and cost.

Data Management Platform

DMPs are helping marketers create a more

holistic, complete and actionable customer profile. According to David Booth of MarTech Today, DMP's are "enabling organizations to build proprietary audience segments to activate data and report across communications channels — including websites, social media, paid media and more — DMPs can deliver a unified perspective on customer interactions leveraging first-, second- or third-party data." By unifying customer data, marketers can focus on the right customer segments.

CRM

Maintaining a single, central database of contacts across marketing, sales, etc. keeps a single record of communication. Various tools enable marketers the ability to bring in data and integrate website content and engagement, social media, analytics, e-commerce, chat, email, phone conversations, etc.

Customer data from CRM's can be critical for personalization across various communication channels. There's a wide spectrum of options from personalized content within emails based on the specific recipient to websites that are dynamically customized to speak to specific customers. Marketing tools that exchange information with CRM databases, can provide valuable insights on how all of the stages of the customer's lifecycle connect—from the initial point of awareness to the point of advocacy and re-purchase.

Email Signature Control

In a smaller example, tools like SenderGen can

help marketers ensure all internal employees are using the same signatures and provide unique messaging within each email they deliver.

Integrated Communications

Disjointed messaging and creative in communications produces less impact. For copy, graphics, video and voice to accurately compliment each other and cohesively align to a brand's voice, tone and story, they must rely on strong written guidelines and detailed inspection. (See 'brand guidelines' and 'campaign definitions')

Action Items

Alignment and integration is an important step. Here are some ways to get started or refine processes:

❑ Set-up cross-functional meetings to establish clear and shared definitions.

❑ Audit your technology stack to discover ways to more tightly integrate data.

❑ Move to a one-stop shop technology platform, where appropriate.

❑ Establish regular meetings with functions like sales to uncover meaningful ways to collaborate.

❑ Seek out tools and technology that empowers other functional areas.

❑ Identify solutions that can be impacted with tighter integration.

❑ Use technology or other means to create a consistent approval process.

❑ Ensure your marketing assets are unified across all channels. Develop the tools to ensure consistency.

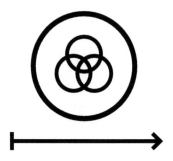

SIMPLIFY to STRENGTHEN ATTENTION

Small disciplines repeated with consistency every day lead to great achievements gained slowly over time.

John C. Maxwell

Manual processes, planning redundancies, bloated techology stacks and a lack of standardization can lead to unnecessary complexity. This can becoming crippling for marketing and focuses attention not on value delivery but on the mechanisms of delivery itself. This can slow down execution, create misalignment on objectives and create other ineffeciencies and waste.

Go Lean

In parallel to hypothesis-driven testing, applying lean principles to marketing involves proving smaller tests first before scaling efforts.

Marketers should determine their Minimum Viable Approach (MVA), which is essentially the end result with the highest return on investment and lowest risk. This is typically coupled with using an agile management framework, discussed in greater detail in the section, "Agile Marketing." Here's an example, incorporating the hypothesis-driven approach from the last section:

- **Hypothesis:** "As a [target audience] I can't find [product or service] when I use a search engine."
- **MVA:** One search ad, targeting one location, using a few keywords and minimal budget.

When the MVA is proven, various multi-variate or A/B tests can be conducted to test ad

Simplify to Strengthen Attention

performance. As new discoveries are made, additional ads, more locations, additional keywords and budget can be increased. Ads that produce more revenue, customer data, impressions or other intended outcomes, will be given a higher quality of execution gradually over time. If value is delivered or proven, the activity is re-tested at greater scale.

Automate

Look for areas to reduce or eliminate manual procedures. First, create lists of workflows and processes. Then, look for processes that can be eliminated and edited, before considering automation. Finally, leverage your existing or new technology to automate. AI-enabled technology can further enhance automation, whereby workflows and processes aren't simply replaced by human-defined bots, but are autonomously discovered based on learned patterns.

Ultimately, complex human processes can be reduced to a simpler series of tasks to get work done. However, a cautionary note is that seeking automation, for the sake of automation without carefully considering how to refine current processes and systems can conversely increase complexity.

Simplify Messaging

Be careful not to overdo your messaging. Too many messages, conflicting messages can can create customer confusion. Audit all your messaging across all various channels to understand what's resonating and what's not.

Find your value proposition (discussed in a later chapter) and strip out the the fluff to create a cohesive and clear story across all channels.

Remove Clutter

Every system and process needs regular housecleaning. Look for ways to delayer your management structures. Take time to 'weed and prune' the junk that has accumulated in your customer management, analytics, advertising and project management systems.

Standardize

By defining common tasks and processes, marketers can reduce variability and deliver greater efficiency. Standardization helps simplify new projects as most of the work has already been done, allowing for additional opportunities to automate and further simplify efforts.

Reduce Waste

Identify areas where waste can be minimized. Typical problems that can introduce wasteful practices into marketing include :

- **Over-production** - Too many activities or things produced with no clear plan on how to utilize them effectively. Additionally, effective campaigns are re-invented, instead of recycled.

- **Over or Under Capacity** - A result of too many or too few people involved in delivering. Too few can result in under-specialized resources spending too much time to complete tasks.

- **Poor Communication** - An over hierarchical communication structure can make it very difficult to take action quickly. This lack of flexibility can cause waste in the form of missed opportunities and unnecessary inaction.

- **Excessive Guesswork** - While trial and error is necesssary in marketing, too much without use of data and evidence creates wasted time, effort and money.

- **Mis-managed Spend** - Lack of understanding where costs can be removed completely from current or future spending.

Reduce Complexity

Audit your existing marketing ecosystem to

understand where complex systems may get in the way of executing:

- How long does it take to get campaigns and marketing materials approved?
- How many are part of the approval process and how are those approvals provided?
- Are there backlogs in the ideation, creation, approval, development, quality control or other areas of execution of marketing activities?
- Do items get lost in email chains?
- Is there difficulty tracking latest version of marketing materials?
- Is there difficulty in maintaining legal compliance?

Streamline Relationships

Working with a number of vendors, contractors, freelancers, partners, suppliers and solution providers can create disjointed software systems and fragmented communication. Look for solutions that help to streamline resource communication, such as WorkMarket.

Also, seek ways to rationalize partner or provider portfolios, and/or recalibrate business relationships. It may be time to consolidate or improve vendor integration processes. Balance all-in-one solutions with best-in-breed to establish the right mix of partner relationships with management simplicity.

Simplify Planning

It may be possible to turn the strategic plan

mentioned in a previous chapter into a one-page marketing plan, supported by additional materials if necessary. While it depends on the size, industry and state of your business or organization, the following might be included in your single-page plan:

- Purpose and ideal customer
- Positioning and differentiation
- Platform strategy
- Promotion strategy
- Conversion strategy
- Growth strategy
- Referrral strategy
- Transaction value strategy
- Retention strategy

Revisit the Plan

Gone are the days of the heavily documented, 5 year plan. Instead, creating a 12-month living document of activities and initiatives can help keep marketing on track. It may outline specific activities by quarter and should be revisited every few months to address business changes and new opportunities. Also monitor pre-defined performance objectives in the plan to determine level of success. Put revisiting the plan in the calendar.

Simplify Technology

- **Eliminate unnecessary marketing technologies.** Find tools or technologies that are not actively utilized.
- **Simplify the technology stack where possible.** Rationalize your portfolio of technologies after getting the quick wins.

Consolidate and reduce the number of solutions while retaining support for marketing business requirements.

- **Utilize the tools and technologies already available within the organization.** Underutilization is typically tied to inadequate training, unclear ownership or staffing. Assess the utilization of current tools and invest in the staffing and training needed to maximize the value of current technologies.

- **Standardize on platforms and tools.** Standardize the technologies themselves and leverage technology to templatize projects, campaigns, reports and other aspects of marketing operations.

- **Renegotiate technology licensing agreements.** Actively review your

Simplify to Strengthen Attention

technology portfolio every year, and renegotiate licensing relationships to focus on alignment with core marketing goals.

Action Items

Not having a sustained effort around an initiative is often having a lack of focus. Try some of these things:

- ❏ Build in an approach to evaluate new technologies, strategies and initiatives that considers their 'MVA'
- ❏ Identify processes that can use automation to scale
- ❏ Audit messaging across channels for the purpose of simplifying
- ❏ Audit various systems for junk and clutter
- ❏ Create a system for how processes can be

standardized

- ❑ Identify areas of waste and create action plan to remove

- ❑ Explore ways to reduce complexity in relationships with vendors, agencies and suppliers

- ❑ Create simplified one-page strategic plans that address the essential needs of each area of marketing

- ❑ Diagram the technology stack and identify areas for consolidation, reduction and better integration

EVOLVE to ADAPT to CHANGE

The best way to thrive in a world that's changing is to change.

– Seth Godin

Two of the biggest enemies to focus are time and change. Shifting priorities, boredom, shiny object syndome, etc. can diminish marketing's ability to 'stick with it' on certain strategies and tactics over time. The related efforts applied to filtering, organizing, controlling, aligning and evolving marketing efforts then become unfruitful as discipline to sustain these activities wane.

Simply put, as efforts on an initiative lessens, so does its focus.

Change can equally delute focus as market shifts, competitive plays, organizational transitions, etc. can become distractions. Change is enevitable. But, it shouldn't be a precursor to total abandonment of a marketing team's strategic direction. Instead, it may simply require adapting targets to better align with the change.

Change doesn't always require an absolute change in focus. It's more often maintaining the current course of action, while making small adaptations or corrections over time.

Complete course correcting too often can lead to wasted time and energy. However, a focus on outdated and irrelevant practices may not produce the expected results. Both don't allow for enough time to establish, scale and sustain enough of the right value delivery that drive results for internal and external customers (more on this in the next chapter).

Instead, in order to successfully sustain marketing activities that can have an impact on the long-term performance of an organization, marketing needs to employ proper planning, competency development, asset maintenance, auditing and benchmarking.

Levels of Maturity

Viewing marketing in terms of its level of maturity as compared to other organizations provides a roadmap of stages in which to improve, aspire and evolve to. There are a number of different frameworks as developed by Gartner and others, but typically the various stages of maturity, which can be applied to various areas within marketing such as data & analytics, customer experience, social, mobile, search, planning & forecasing, marketing technology, etc, include ad-hoc, repeatable, defined, integrated and automated, and optimized.

Ad-hoc or Underdeveloped

In this stage, there are few defined or formal processes. There's also minimal consistency from the individual, team or organization in the implementation of marketing activities.

Repeatable

This is when successful practices are repeated and planning is based on the success of other initiatives. Eventually, as these activities are repeated, the organization will begin to get more proficient with those particular activities.

Defined

Documented processes, including those at a managerial and operational level, help marketing to perform more efficiently. Taking into account industry best practices and organized into a cohesive set of well-understood, integrated processes, they can be adjusted over time when appropriate. Also, metrics and KPI's as to which to evaluate performance will be more clearly defined.

Integrated and Automated

Platforms are connected to each other such as content management systems, marketing automation systems, social API's, customer relationship management, analytics API's, etc. There is also a greater cohesive customer experience across all channels and better strategic integration with other functions of the organization.

Optimized

World-class marketing teams operate at this level. Marketing is viewed as a critical function of the organization and marketing is heavily tied to revenue performance and other important strategic measures. Advanced techniques are deployed including personalization, multivariate testing, full-fledged agile management, advanced workflow automation, etc.

Maturity Matrix

Create a marketing maturity matrix to better understand where you stand in each area. Plot out these stages as five columns (or appropriate number of stages for your organization) and the key areas of focus in your marketing function as the rows (ie. data and analytics, email marketing, website optimization, etc.). Then define each stage within each area of focus, or simply use a broader stage-level definition. Finally, start to identify your levels of maturity for each area of focus.

Forbes has used a relatively granular approach for their marketing maturity and accountability model and has areas such as functional and role alignment, common funding practices, measurement skills and competencies, and collective growth rewards and incentives. Their marketing leadership then defines these under three levels: basic, advanced and best-in-class.

Now with a bird's-eye view of maturity levels, begin to determine some activities or initiatives that can be added to the backlog as discussed in FILTERING.

Continuous improvement means that the organization is always rising higher, with no absolute upper limit.

Hypothesis-Driven Decisions

While data-driven marketing has been around for decades, insight-driven marketing is still an emerging concept. It involves applying scientific principles to the experimentation process. Thinking about every action, task or project as an experiment that requires acquiring knowledge, testing and iterative change, can often help predict future outcomes and validate assumptions with some certainty. Of course, anything dealing with human behavior is far from being predictable. This isn't data for the sake of data, but data for the purpose of driving better results. A hypothesis requires: a presumed problem, proposed solution and anticipated results. For example,

- **Problem Statement:** "The conversion process is too long, causing unnecessary friction."
- **Proposed Solution:** "Shorten the number of steps from 3 to 2."
- **Anticipated Results:** "Decrease the

drop-off rate."

Thus, the hypothesis might be clearly stated as "The conversion process is too long, causing unnecessary friction, and therefore if we shorten the number of steps from 3 to 2 we will decrease the drop-off rate."

Filtering various approaches through hypothesis testing provides a structured approach to make decisions based on evidence, not guess-work.

Marketing Enablement

According to Forrester, 96% of CMOs have stated that their departments are being asked to do things it has never been asked to do before. Thar's why marketing needs training and support that adapts. This includes not only field-specific material, but also company and industry relevant topics.

Some of the areas to address include:

- Training on new tools and technology
- Education on products and services
- Sales insights and data collection
- Decision-making authority

Product & Solution Training

Ensure all staff in the organization is operating off of one set of materials on products, services and offerings. A central knowledgebase is crucial for giving marketing a single source of information, even if only in its raw form. Additionally, provide opportunities for ongoing hands on training, whether through participating in front line conversations with customers or meetings with engineering teams.

Technology Training

With the rapid pace of technology changes, provide ongoing training and education on solutions available in the market. Conferences, workshops, and online training classes can provide opportunities to learn best practices, share ideas with peers and build more advanced knowledge on toolsets.

Talent Development

Without the right people on board with the right skills, maintaining focus on your set of initiatives becomes difficult. Some new activities may require additional training and development. Alternatively, it could mean hiring the appropriate external team of consultants, agencies or contractors. Develop an ongoing plan to improve a team's skillset with continuing education that deepens knowledge in high priority areas.

In general, a strategy to hire and train the right marketing talent may include working with HR partners, external agencies or internal team members and executives to craft the right programs. You'll likely need to cover these areas:

- **Talent Acquisition** - Source candidates and create a hiring process that closes the deal. What is it about your team that is different, special or unique? Is your marketing organization being sought after in the marketplace? When does it make sense to outsource talent to utilize in-house resources?

- **Business Alignment** - Build an onboarding program and informal or formal performance evaluation process to ensure continuing alignment of performance with business objectives. Outside of the typical onboarding process, how are staff members onboarded into new roles and new opportunities.

- **Learning and Development** - Create regular opportunities that improve competency and capability for high achievement. Ensure a regular cadence exists around skill and knowledge development. Survey team members to understand where gaps exist, provide outside opportunities for growth and connect people around both common and uncommon areas of knowledge. Management should be developing new leaders in the marketing function by offloading more administrative tasks and providing opportunities to stretch knowledge and growth.

- **Retention** – Ensure team satisfaction by creating roles that provide opportunities for personal growth and development and compensation models that compete in the market. Create an envionrment where honest feedback is welcomed and accepted, and build anonymous channels for feedback, as well as multiple channels for feedback.

Be sure to include each or some of these

activities in the filtering and prioritization process. You'll want to identify the gaps in each and what should be prioritized. Impact could be measured by understanding how top-performing candidates are sourced, common areas or attributes that resulted in staff to leave or methods team members prefer to learn. Developing and keeping good talent, in-house or outsourced, will help sustain marketing efforts, and minimize constraints from poor personnel performance, capacity deficencies or sudden gaps in capabilities.

Content Strategies

As content development continues to serve as the cornerstone to marketing strategy and the quantity of content continues to rise in the marketplace, especially in B2B, a focus on several strategies can ensure sustainability. Think of content around how it can evolve into different formats and serve as pillars of focus in a content strategy.

Evergreen Content

Evergreen content is designed to last for a long time and typically takes a longer or larger form. Some example types which may include a variety of media formats include:

- Case Studies

- Stats and Data

- Product Reviews

- How To Guides

- Beginner's Guides

- Lists

Thoroughly researched topics retains relevance and continues to attract an audience over time.

Repurposed Content

Given the demands on producing content in both higher qualities and quantities and in a greater variety of formats, efforts to recycle existing content can save time and effort and provide more usable content over time. This can open up more time to focus on distribution, analysis and strategy. It begins with developing a large piece of content, which might take the form of an e-book, guide or presentation. It's then repurposed into other forms of content such as blogs, webinars, videos, slideshares, etc. Often these smaller forms of content are intended to lead the audience to the cornerstone piece of content intended to generate leads.

User-Generated Conent

Often used in Ecommerce, user-generated content is an important play that generates a steady stream of content from external sources. Additionally, the life of content can be extended by leveraging it alongside related products and categories. Similar to evergreen content, the idea is ultimately to extend the life of your content assets.

Process Improvement

Evaluating processes for improvement and automation will increase efficiency. Even creative teams can learn to focus on streamlining workflow. Make part of your meeting agenda to discuss solutions for automation and process improvement. Start with a few things to measure, examine the results and brainstorm ways to reduce the time to complete a task or improve the quality of a given result. Here are a few broader measures to improve processes:

- Consider moving to a paperless environment with the use of online proofing and collaboration tools like ProofHQ to get approvals done faster.

- Leverage automation workflows to deliver timely information. See the section on 'Automation.'

- Use repeatable processes when planning, executing and examining activities. See section on 'Agile Management.'

- Create a central database of documented processes for repeatability, consistency and examination for refinement.

- Use time tracking software to measure categories of time spent and look for ways to structure.

- Find technology solutions or service partners that can eliminate lower value activities or areas of lower competency internally.

Trends and Market Shifts

As consumer preferences change, so should marketing efforts. However, don't invest in new technology, people or processes, if its not going to benefit your business. To avoid getting too distracted by shifting trends:

- Create a strategy to identify the latest innovations that may align best with your marketing objectives

- Assess the resources available to procure the technology you are looking for and find out which one of them will work for you

- Dedicate some efforts and time to evaluate the usefulness of a particular technology before implementing it full-scale

- Keep to budgeting rules set, and adjust as necessary.

- Experiment with new mediums, tools, etc. using the 5, 10 or 20% allocation or resources and test them to evaluate performance.

Action Items

Not having a sustained effort around an initiative is often having a lack of focus. Try some of these things:

❑ Create a culture and mind-set of continuous

process improvement. Seek to create repeatable processes and systems on a daily basis.

❑ Hold meetings with a regular cadence and structure. Even if they're short of lack a lot of substance, the cadence keeps the ball moving.

❑ Enable your team to grow and improve through training.

❑ Plan and decide on how to report, on what, how often and when.

❑ Develop strategies, using content for example, that create lasting and long-term opportunities to recycle and repurpose without the need to reinvent.

❑ Plan for ongoing audits, or opportunities to step back and examine your progress.

❑ Define a roadmap for where to take your

marketing function.

- ❑ Seek places to integrate and automate software and systems or other ways to do your job, even when you're not doing it.

- ❑ Revisit your annual and quarterly plans.

- ❑ Set benchmarks and how long to achieve them.

- ❑ Monitor market trends and shifts and find ways to adapt.

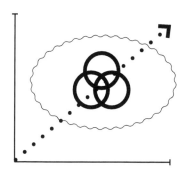

DELIVER for *CUSTOMER VALUE*

Marketing is not the art of finding clever ways to dispose of what you make. It is the art of creating genuine customer value.

– Philip Kotler

The center of focus of all marketing efforts is delivering value to both external and internal customers. Marketing's unique 360-degree view of external and internal customers should create a bi-directional, and exponential flow of value creation. Internal customers can be empowered with marketing's customer and market knowledge; helping them to create better products, deliver better service or make better operational decisions. On the other hand, external customers can be provided with solution knowledge and impactful omni-channel experiences, products and services that improve their daily lives.

The challenge, however, is getting all of the marketing engine cylinders firing and similtaneously focused on exceptional value creation across the business and marketplace. Often marketing professionals, executives and teams can fall prey to delivering gimicks, stand-alone campaigns, miopic promotional efforts, unnecessary or unimpactful technology or channel capabilities, etc.

Competing priorities, unclear objectives, shiny object syndrome, lack of customer or market intelligence, etc. can cause marketing to focus on lower value activities.

Marketing must examine activities, initiatives and strategies that don't align to certain defined value drivers in an impactful way. Those identified should be de-prioritized or eliminated. This can be difficult. Sometimes it means ignoring popular promotional channels, re-examining product line and messaging strategies, re-aligning staff, re-configuring teams, adjusting budgets, etc.

This is where the rubber meets the road. As discussed in the previous chapters, efforts around prioritization, organization, process control, change management, and simplification should all work together to enable marketers to not only focus on efforts that truly produce value, but also enable them to deliver more.

Customer Perceived Value

How successful marketing is at promoting, selling and distributing an offer or offering, largely depends on whether customers believe it satisfies their wants and needs. Moreover, it's the difference between the total obtained benefits a customer perceives they are receiving and the total costs they perceive they are paying. This simple equation can be written as:

$$PV = TPV - TPC$$
Percieved Value = Total Perceived Value - Total Perceived Costs

The idea of "perception" is important here. It's marketing's job to help shape and increase a customer's perceived value for products and services. This chapter serves to provide some ideas around how to do that.

External Customer Value

First, and foremost ensure a prospective buyer's perceived value of an organization's product and/or service is maximized. Some of these components of external customer value include:

- Combination of value attributes
- Cost benefits
- Problem & solution knowledge
- Delightful & cohesive experiences

Value Attributes

According to a recent study published in the Harvard Business Review by Eric Almquist, John Senior, and Nicolas Bloch of Bain Consulting, there are 30 ways to create customer value. While all functions of an organization participate in creating, refining and delivering these value attributes, marketing plays an important role in defining and shaping them.

Not only should these be used for informing product and service design, but also for any "offer" or "experience" marketing might deliver: communication, advertisements, content, in-store experience design, ecommerce functionality, etc.

While they vary in importance by industry and market, the right levels and combination of functional values produces differentiation in the market and desired appeal to customers.

Functional Values

- **Reduce effort** - How well does your offering reduce the amount of time and energy to complete a task or series of tasks?

- **Avoid hassle** - Is your offering convienent, easy-to-use and accessible? How does it help a customer avoid painful experiences?

- **Reduce cost** - Does your offering help customers reduce expenses?

- **Quality** - What materials are being used, what is the combination of those materials and how does it hold up against competitiors?

- **Variety** - Is there a number of options to choose from in the total product offering?

- **Sensory appeal** - Does your offering appeal to a customer's sense of smell, hearing or touch?

- **Informs** - Does it help make customers smarter?

- **Saves time** - Are there ways it can reduce time to get a job done?
- **Simplifies** - Does it reduce complexity?
- **Makes money** - Can it increase wealth?
- **Reduce risk** - Are there ways it can protect a customer from loss - financial, psychological or other?
- **Organizes** - Can it help reduce clutter or mess?
- **Connects** - Can it connect people in a meaningful way?
- **Wellness** - Does it provide physical and mental health?
- **Therapeutic value** - Can it enhance well-being?
- **Fun & entertainment** - Is it gamified or provide other exciting appeal?
- **Attractiveness** - Does it help people feel more attractive?
- **Provides access** - Does it give exclusive

access to certain benefits?

- **Reduces anxiety** - Are there benefits that reduce stress in the buying experience or offer itself?
- **Rewards me** - Does it reinforce behaviors?
- **Nostalgia** - Does it provide a sense of
- **Design and Aesthetics** - Does it evoke emotional satisfaction from its specific design?
- **Badge value** - Is there a perception that it gives an elevated status?
- **Motivation** - Does it help drive goal achievement?
- **Heirloom** - Is it long-lasting or help provide for future generations?
- **Affiliation and belonging** - Does it help people feel like part of a group or community?
- **Provides hope** - Does it give something to be optimistic about?

- **Self-actualization –** Is it providing a sense of personal accomplishment or improvement?
- **Self-transcendence** – Is it helping society at large?

A survey the authors also conducted confirmed that companies that were identified with more of these values also had better performance.

Companies that could claim four or more value elements had, on average, three times the Net Promoter Score (NPS) of companies that focused on just one customer value, and 20 times the NPS of companies with none. Additionally, companies that scored high on four or more value elements had recent revenue growth four times greater than that of companies with only one high score.

By leveraging customer and competitive intelligence, marketing can work with product and service teams to prioritize value attribute creation and enhancement projects. For example, if I know that 'affiliation' is most important to customers, could more investment be focused on programs that establish a sense of community around the product? Ultimately, it's about finding those key elements to focus on, and adjusting time and resource investments accordingly. Additionally, it requires ensuring there's alignment across channels as it relates to these elements of value.

Delightful and Cohesive Experiences

An extension of your product or service, or

arguably, an interwoven part of your offering, experiences encapsulate the end-to-end journey a customer takes when engaging with your organization throughout the buyer's journey.

Experiential marketing focused on producing outcomes has to be intense, and not simply pleasurable. There are generally two areas to examine in your marketing: the components of an experience and the associated attributes that can make them delightful.

A study in the Eurpoean Management Journal by Chiara Gentile, Nicola Spiller and Giuliano Noci suggests that the customer experience has six components that can be explored by marketers:

- **Sensorial Component** – stimulates the senses as sight, hearing, touch, taste and smell in order to generate aesthetical pleasure, satisfaction, sense of beauty.

- **Emotional Components** – stimulates feelings, emotions and moods reaching the affective system with the aim of creating an emotional relation with the company, brand or products

- **Cognitive Component** – stimulates thoughts, conscious mental processes and creativity which can make customers revise assumptions of products

- **Pragmatic Component** – stimulates acting, use of something. It is not restrictive to the post purchase stage but to all the product's lifecycle stages

- **Lifestyle Component** – stimulates people's

values and beliefs through the adoption of lifestyle and behaviours

- **Relational Components** – stimulates relationships, social life, communities, social identity, related to the previous component

Cost Benefits

Because of the level of importance of cost as a component of your total value proposition, it needs its own consideration. Types of cost to consider can include:

- **Monetary cost** – this refers specifically to the cost of purchasing and maintaining an offering.

- **Time cost** – consumers are becoming increasingly busy and time poor. The amount of time required to buy, assemble, learn, use, maintain, etc. can play a factor.

- **Physical cost** - outside of the time required to buy and support a product or service, there may be physical effort to do so also.

- **Psychological cost** - uncertainty around the purchase and support of products and services can create risk in a buyer's mind. Additionally, there may be mental effort required.

Marketers that seek to try and reduce these perceived and actual costs to potential buyers, will improve the perception of the value attributes previously discussed.

Problem and Solution Education

Advertising, marketing's most well-known function, plays an important role, not only for the business in terms of driving customer awareness, acquisition and brand loyalty, but for society at large.

John Calfee, a leading advertising scholar, has argued alongside other economic scholars that markets with advertising are far superior to markets without advertising, and makes two strong points as to why:

- It's an "efficient and sometimes irreplaceable mechanism for bringing consumers information" that they would otherwise not have.
- It helps to generate "more and better information [that] also generates ripple effects in the market. These include enhanced incentives to create new information and

develop better products."

The key is to focus your paid, owned and earned media on your most important product strengths and value attributes. It ultimately helps customers understand and solve problems. Some excellent examples include Volvo's video commercial using storytelling to show you a path to self-actualization in "The Get Away Car," or similarly Patagonia's Vote our Planet hub, a collection of content and resources around environmental news and guides, guiding you down a journey to self-transcendence.

Think about the connected story all of your awareness-driving activities as opportunities to help customers solve problems, get inspired, be entertained, feel nostalgic, etc. And be absolutely intentional about connecting the dots to your offerings central theme. Make these activities extensions of the value your product or service already provides.

Internal Customer Value

Delivering customer value also includes considering internal customers like employees, team members, executives, departments, suppliers, agencies, etc. Here are six areas of focus for where your marketing efforts can produce more value to the organization:

- Brand stewardship and equity
- Customer equity
- Voice of the market and customer intelligence
- Organizational competence

- Offering innovation
- Growth platform development

Brand Stewardship and Equity

Brand equity is a long-term game. It can help to contribute and drive future in-market demand performance. According to the BrandDynamics™ pyramid, there are five drivers to brand equity including:

- **Presence** - the extent of a brand's presence in the market
- **Relevance** - the extent to which an offering is relevant and appealing to consumers
- **Performance** - fulfillment of basic functional promise
- **Advantage** - perceived advantages over competitors

Deliver for Customer Value

- **Bonding** - a brand's ability to generate loyal customers

Thinking outside of shorter-term marketing mix tactics and how marketing can have an impact on brand equity through these drivers, marketers can impact long-term financial performance. Branding Strategy Insider suggests measuring brand equity using these three metrics:

- **Knowledge Metrics** - Do customers or prospective customers know and understand what your product or service actually does? Do they know of the value they'll get from using it? Do they perhaps have a misguided or misunderstood sense of its functions and/or value?

- **Preference Metrics** – How is your company perceived in the market? Is the brand relevant and aligned to its values, is it accessible to the market, does it create an emotional connection and, lastly, how does it compare from a cost/benefit perspective?

- **Financial Metrics** – What's the percentage of overall sales in your industry that your market takes in? What's the price you offer your product or service for? What's your company's ability to offer your product or service for a higher-than-average price to increase its appeal? What's the amount of money your company has made by selling products or services, and the potential revenue to be made if trends continue? What's your company's ability to scale as revenue increases?

To adequetely measure brand equity on a regular basis, you have to decide what factors to focus on. Then consider what ways to measure, both quantitatively and quantitatively. Find ways to gauge sentiment through ongoing customer surveys that allow you to compare results on an annual basis to understand what's changed. Use reference points in your questions, such as: 'rate how you understand the products we sell on a scale of 1-5.' This will allow more intagible questions around emotional connection or satisfaciton to be quantified and compared over time.

Voice of the Market

Marketers can improve the perceived value being created by conducting qualitative and quantitative customer research in order to:

- Validate the points of value creation identified. Are the methods we use to position and sell products resonating in the market?

- Determine new dimensions of value creation. Are there areas to create new elements of value?

- Assess the relative importance of each dimension of value from a customer's perspective. Does what we preceive as valueable matter to the customer?

Organizational Competence

If the size of your organization is one or many, others in leadership, engineering, sales and finance will need to be educated according to the knowledge that marketing can provide: voice of the customer, product/market fit, effective messaging and content, customer acquisition costs, etc. Marketing should create streamlined and repeatable methods to educate others in the organization on these areas of importance.

Innovation

Innovating products, services, campaigns and other offers is done effectively with marketing's ability to help establish desirability, feasibility and viability. Marketing has a bird's eye view on a customer needs and desires. It can work with other teams to understand feasibility. And it can use data to help craft the case for an innovation's viability to produce results for the business and add value to the customer.

The point here is that marketing can and should provide a leading role in ushering in innovative systems, technology and ideas to an organization. Particularily, those innovate projects that have potential to deliver value to internal and external customers. The key is to paint a clear picture of where marketing will 'play in the sandbox.'

Growth Platform Development

Essentially, a platform is a strategy to mobilize and empower an ecosystem, not merely a technology. Examples of strategic growth platforms which in these cases are using specific and innovative product areas or entering into a new distribution channel:

- In order to increase growth, Apple

Computers targeted "personal music systems" using its personal business of computers

- IBM invented the term "e-business" and used it as the organizing theme of what the company did during the late 1990s

Value Communication

As the primary function for broadcasting the various elements of an offering's value into the market, marketing should seek to use a balanced communication approach to ensure that all facets are perceived favorably by the customer.

- **Emphasize the benefits** - All the benefits a customer receives according to the value attributes as defined previously

- **Emphasize the favourable differences** - All favourable points with which an offer is distinguised from the competition (the unique selling proposition or USP)

- **Emphasize the critical value factors** - No more than two buying advantages to sure there is clarity in the offer

- **Emphasize the threshold removers** - Possible purchase thresholds are removed as a result of which the customer is convinced to choose for the product/ service.

Journey Value Optimization

There are essentially three ways to grow a business: acquire new customers, increase the transaction value per customer or increase the number of transactions per customer. As popularized by Digital Marketer, the Customer

Value Optimization process involves improving various steps within the marketing and sales funnel in order to move each of those levers for the business.

The goal is to provide additional incremental value to the customer at each stage of the customer journey.

An approach commonly referenced in the digital marketing space, specifically B2B companies, includes building on these 5 steps:

- Lead Magnet – a valuable piece of information given in exchange for contact information
- Tripwire Offer – an offer (product, service, content, etc) with a lower barrier to purchase

(cost, risk, etc.)

- Core Offer - these are primary products and services
- Profit Maximizer - cross sell and upsell opportunities
- Return Path - tactics used to segment engaged prospects and re-engage with relevant messaging

Action Items

Constantly revisit the ways in which marketing communicates and delivers value. Try some of these things:

❑ Cross-reference the value attributes list against campaigns, messaging, experiences, products and services. Determine areas where new attributes can be added or existing ones reinforced.

- ❑ Use journey maps and other CX management tools to understand the components and attributes across marketing channels that create delightful experiences, not simply pleasurable ones.

- ❑ Examine all the types of costs incurred by customers to buy and use products and services.

- ❑ Brainstorm ways in marketing channels the brand's story can be better woven together to educate customers

- ❑ Consider establishing a regular means to measure brand equity

- ❑ Establish a regular cadance of delivering tailored customer intelligence data to others in the organization

- ❑ Uncover ways marketing messages, channels

and experiences can be shaped to better tell the value story

❑ Establish a system for introducing innovation projects and growth platform development into marketing initiatives and programs

❑ As a B2B marketer, look for opportunities to incrementally increase value delivery to move customers through their journey

Micro Moments

While the FOCUSED framework applies to a general holistic approach and perspective on marketing management, it can also be used at a micro-level. For example, when running a campaign:

- Channels and priorities will need evaluated and filtered (Filter)
- Experts and teams will need to organized and plans created (Organize)
- Tools will need to provide reliable measurements on campaign success, budgets established and methodologies in place to manage activities and outcomes (Control)
- Stakeholders will need to be aligned such as front line service representatives, sales team

members and production teams (Unify)

- Messaging may need simplified across channels (Simplify)
- Plans will need to be in place with ongoing meetings to take measurements and make adjustments to maintain momentum (Evolve)
- Value attributes may need to be properly defined to ensure that the right value proposition is communicated (Deliver)

Made in the USA
Columbia, SC
11 July 2020